Buildings

Todd Mercer

Contents

Buildings for Different Purposes 2
Who Designs Buildings? 4
Meet an Architect 9
Making Buildings Strong and Stable 12
Building for the Environment 14
Unusual Buildings 18
Design-a-Building Challenge 20
Questions 22
Glossary 23
Index 24

Buildings for Different Purposes

People build buildings for many different purposes. For example, your school was built so students would have a place where they could come together to learn.

Look at the pictures on this page and the next page. What is the purpose of each building?

3

Who Designs Buildings?

People who design buildings are called **architects**. The architect's job is to plan what the building will look like. Architects also plan what the building will be like inside.

Let's take a look at how architects design a building.

Step 1: Do Research

Research is the first step in designing a building. Architects may talk to many different people to find out the answers to questions like these:
- What will the building be used for?
- How big does the building need to be?
- Does the building need to have big rooms, small rooms, or some of each?
- Where will the building be built?

Step 2: Make Sketches

After doing research, architects start to make sketches of what the building might look like, both inside and out. They plan how many rooms there will be, what each room will be used for, and where in the building each room will be.

Architects make many sketches to explore many different designs for the building. Then they choose the design that works best for the building's purpose.

Step 3: Create Models

Once architects have chosen a design for the building, they build a **model** that shows what the building will look like. A model is the best way for architects to show others what the finished building will look like.

Step 4: Make Detailed Plans

After the model is built, architects start to make detailed plans of the building. These plans are sometimes called **blueprints**.

The blueprints show exactly how big each room will be and where the heating, electrical, and other systems will go in the building. The blueprints also show the builders how to build the building.

Today, many architects use computers to help them make blueprints.

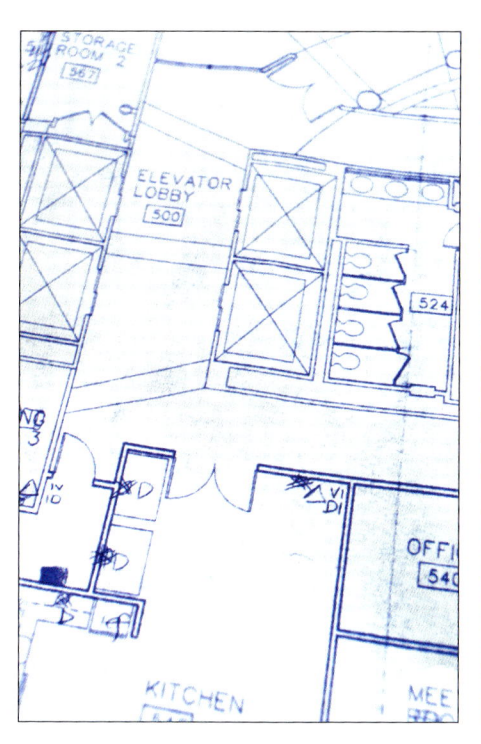

Step 5: Supervise Construction

Architects aren't finished when the blueprints are completed. When construction workers start to build the building, architects supervise the construction to make sure that the builders are following the plans on the blueprint.

Meet an Architect

Mary Ellen Lynch is an architect who works with a group of other architects to create plans for new homes and stores. Sometimes, Mary Ellen also creates plans for people who want to make changes to a home or store that has already been built.

When she was in school, Mary Ellen was very good at art and mathematics. Being an architect allows her to use her talents in both of these subjects.

Read the interview with Mary Ellen to learn how architects design buildings to make them strong.

Interview with Mary Ellen Lynch

Question: What materials do you use to make strong buildings?

Mary Ellen: We use steel and wood in the frames of buildings. We also use concrete. We use wood for smaller buildings such as houses. Steel is used in larger buildings because it is the strongest of these materials. You wouldn't build a large building, like a **skyscraper**, out of wood because the wood is not strong enough.

Question: What shapes do you use in the buildings you design?

Mary Ellen: We use a lot of squares and rectangles. These shapes create good spaces for people to live and work in. Triangles are good strong shapes, but using them would create slanted ceilings.

Question: What do you put in your blueprints to make a building strong?

Mary Ellen: We often use **beams** and **columns**. Beams and columns give the building support.

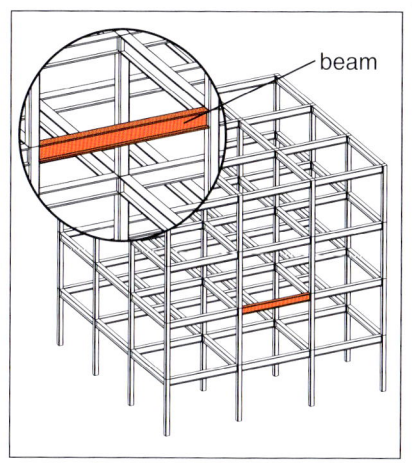

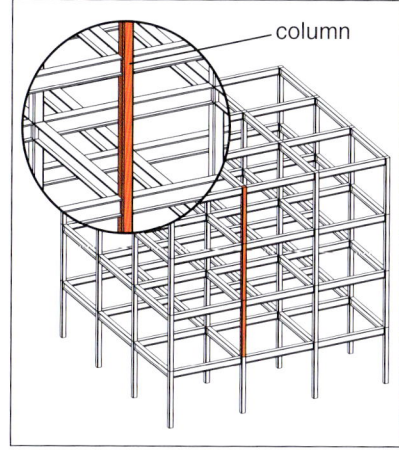

Question: What do you like most about designing buildings?

Mary Ellen: I like the creative process. And it's wonderful to see the final product—a building that people will use.

Making Buildings Strong and Stable

Mary Ellen Lynch talked about how architects use strong materials and strong shapes to make buildings strong. Architects also want to make sure that their buildings are **stable** so they don't wobble or move.

Let's look at some of the shapes and materials architects use in building plans to make sure a building will be stable.

A **strut** is a bar made of metal or wood. It is placed in the **frame** of a building to help the frame support the building's weight. Struts help to make a building strong and stable.

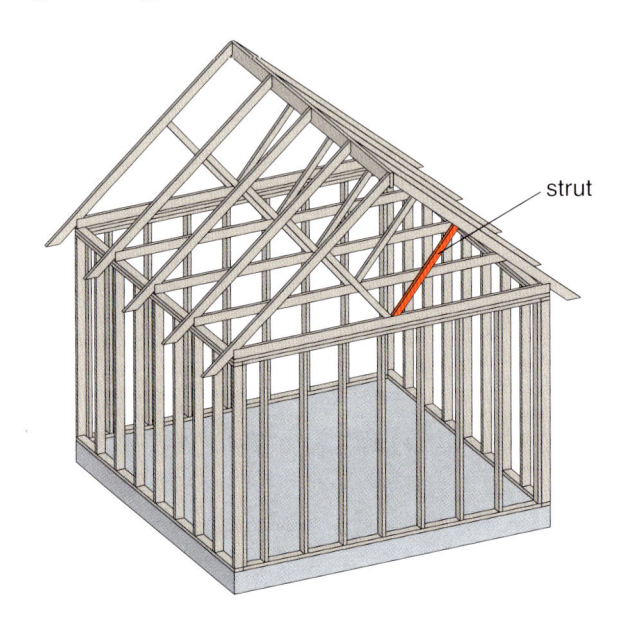

A **tie**, sometimes called a **tie beam**, is a rod or beam that holds parts of the building structure together.

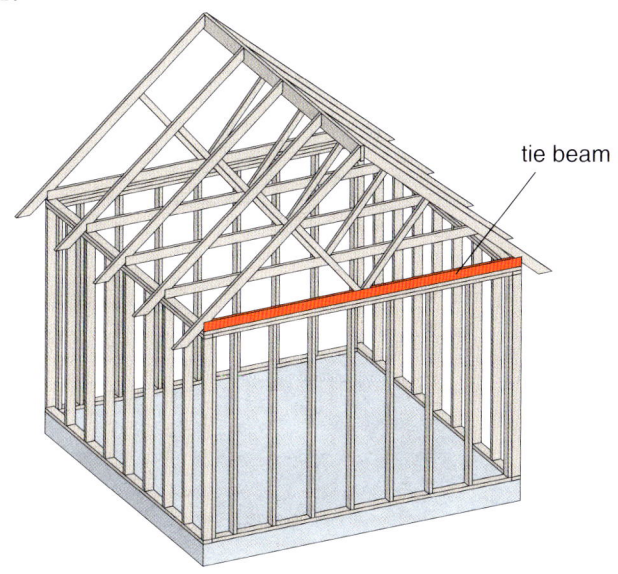

tie beam

A **buttress** can be made of stone, brick, or wood. The buttress is built against a wall to give it more strength.

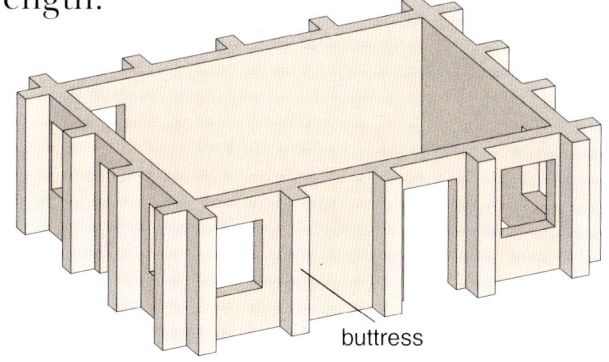

buttress

13

Building for the Environment

When architects plan a building, they need to think about the environment around the building. A building's design has to be right for its environment.

Some buildings are built in areas that get lots of snow. If you've ever shoveled snow, you know that it can be very heavy. Too much snow on a roof can make it collapse.

For areas that get lots of snow, architects often design buildings that have roofs with a steep slope. The slope lets snow slide off the roof.

In some areas of the world, earthquakes often happen. For these areas, architects design buildings to be especially strong so they won't collapse during an earthquake.

Today, we know how to make buildings that are stronger than old buildings. During an earthquake, old buildings sometimes collapse, while many new buildings remain standing.

Most buildings have a **foundation** that is built beneath the ground. That's why construction workers start a building by digging a hole. The foundation is built in the hole.

In areas where the ground is frozen solid all year round, it's impossible to dig a hole for the foundation. So architects design buildings that do not have an underground foundation.

Architects try to use building materials that are available close to the building site. It's more expensive to bring in materials from far away.

In areas where there are lots of forests that provide wood for building, many homes are built of wood.

In some areas, there is lots of clay for making bricks. Brick homes are often built in this area of the country.

Unusual Buildings

Some architects use their imaginations to design buildings that are very different from most designs we see. Take a look at some of these unusual buildings.

This apartment building was built in 1967. People were amazed by its unusual design.

This round house has a motor that allows it to rotate.

It's hard to find a straight line anywhere in this Spanish museum designed by architect Frank Gehry.

This building in Barcelona, Spain, was designed around 1900 by architect Antoni Gaudi.

The design of the Sydney Opera House, in Australia, is famous all around the world. It took 14 years to complete construction.

Design-a-Building Challenge

Now it's your turn to be an architect. Your challenge is to design a portable classroom for your school. Work with a small group.

1. Do Research

Look around your classroom and think about the different ways your classroom is used. Talk to teachers and students about what they would like to see in a design for a classroom.

2. Make Sketches

Sketch different ideas for how the portable classroom might look on the inside and outside. Then choose your best idea.

3. Create a Model

Build a simple model to show your ideas to others. Think about what materials you can use to build your model. You could start with a shoebox, and then draw squares and rectangles to show where desks and tables would go. Remember to include windows and blackboards.

4. Build for Stability

Use craft sticks or other materials to build a frame for your classroom. Think about how you could use struts, ties, and buttresses to make your classroom stable.

Questions

1. What are the four steps architects follow when they design a building? List the steps in order.
2. What three structural supports do architects use to make buildings stable? Explain what each one does.
3. Why do architects think about the environment around a building? List three reasons.
4. What building in your neighborhood do you like best? Explain why you like it.

Glossary

architect a person who designs buildings and supervises their construction

beam a horizontal piece of wood or steel that helps to support weight in a building

blueprints the detailed plans that architects create for a building

buttress a structure built against a wall to give it more strength

column a vertical piece of wood or steel that helps support weight in a building. Columns may also be made from concrete.

foundation the bottom part of a building that the rest of the structure sits on. The foundation is often built into the ground.

frame the "skeleton" of the building, which makes the building strong and stable

model a small version of what a finished building will look like

skyscraper a very tall building

stable doesn't move or change position

strut a metal or wooden bar placed in a building's frame to make it stronger

tie or **tie beam** a rod or beam that holds parts of a building together

Index

architect 4–11
beam 11
blueprints 7
building materials 10, 17
buttress 13
column 11
environment 14–17
models 6
strut 12
tie 13